At the Top of Our Lungs

A Student Worship Choir Collection

As recorded by Puresound Student Worship Ministries
Community Bible Church
San Antonio, TX

lillenas

PUBLISHING COMPANY

lillenas.com

Contents

Hosanna

Words and Music by
BROOKE FRASER
Arr. by Kristen Silvia

6
13
The whole earth shakes, the whole earth shakes.
The peo - ple sing,
Em
1 CD: 2
1
Am
15
(to pg. 5, meas. 10)
2 CD: 3
SOLO cont. on mel.
with CHOIR f
the peo - ple sing.
Ho-san -
mel. f
(to pg. 5, meas. 10)
D
2
Am
D
18
- na, Ho-san - na. Ho - san-na in the high - est.
G/B
C
D
Em
C
Em
f

21
D
G/B
C
D
Em
Ho-san - na, Ho-san - na. Ho-
24
CD: 4
C
D
Em
san - na in the high - est.
27
SOLOS cont. with CHOIR (Female ad lib freely)
3. I see a gen - e - ra - tion,
4. I see a near re - vi - val
G
D/F#

29
ris - ing up to take their place, with self - less faith,
stir - ring as we pray and seek; we're on our knees,
Em
31
1 CD: 5 (to pg. 7, meas. 27) 2 CD: 6
with self - less faith. we're on our knees.
1 (to pg. 7, meas. 27) 2
Am D Am
34
Ho-san - na, Ho-san - na. Ho-
mel.
D G/B C D Em

37
Female SOLO ad lib with CHOIR
san - na in the high - est._____ Ho-san - na, Ho-san-
C   Em   D   G/B   C
40
-na.___ Ho - san - na in the high - est.______
D   Em   C   D   Em   D/F#
43
CD: 7
G   Am   Bm7

10
46
DUET
Male
Heal my heart and make it clean.
Female
Heal my heart and make it clean,
C
D
48
O - pen up my eyes to the things un - seen.
things un - seen,
G
Em
50
CD: 8
Show me how to love like You have loved me.
loved me.
C
D
Em

53
1st time: SOLO only
Ho-san - na, Ho-san - na.__ Ho-
2nd and 3rd time: CHOIR parts
- na, Ho-san - na.__ Ho-
D
G/B
C
D
Em
56
san - na in the high - est.______
Ho-san - na, Ho-san -
2nd & 3rd times: Female SOLO ad lib freely
1st time: add Female SOLO
Ho-san - na, Ho-san -
san - na in the high - est.______
Ho-san - na, Ho-san -
C
Em
D
G/B
C

59
1, 2
- na. Ho - san - na in the high - est.
- na. Ho - san - na in the high - est.
- na. Ho - san - na in the high - est.
D Em C D
61
(to pg. 11, meas. 53)
3
san - na in the high - est.
Female SOLO cont. ad lib freely
(to pg. 11, meas. 53)
3
1st time: Add CHOIR
Ho - san - san - na in the high - est.
(to pg. 11, meas. 53)
3
G C D

SOLOS join CHOIR
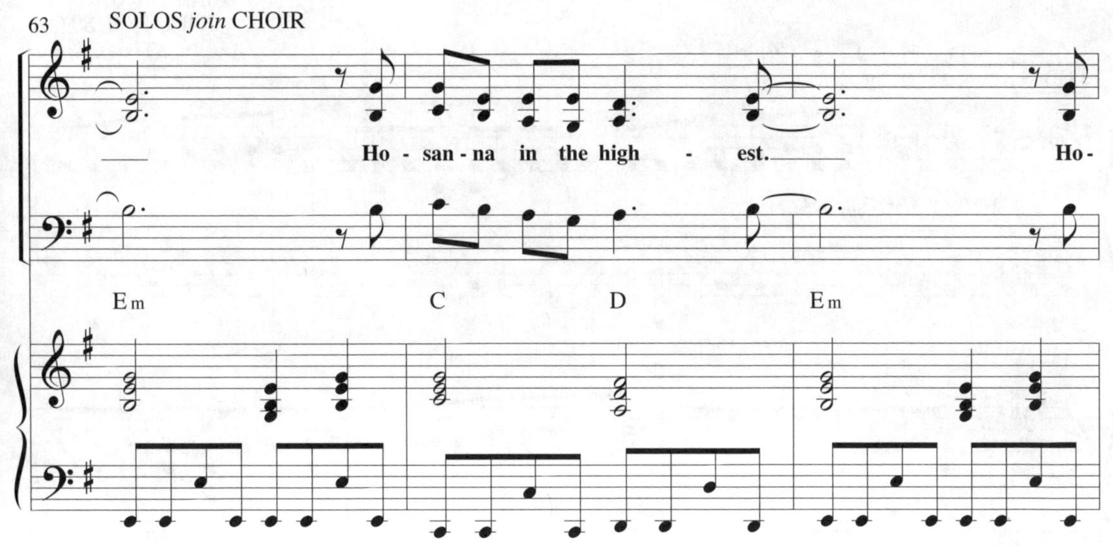
63
Ho - san - na in the high - est. Ho-
Em   C   D   Em

66
san - na in the high - est.
C   D   G   G

Salvation Is Here

Words and Music by
JOEL HOUSTON
Arr. by Kristen Silvia

God a - bove____ all my hopes and____ fears.____
mak - ing____ loud____ our____ free - dom____ songs.____
B (no3)
G#m7
B (no3) / F#
E 2(no3)
CD: 11 2nd time
1st time: Sing Cues
I don't____ care____ what the world throws____ at____ me now,____
All in____ all____ that the world would____ know____ Your name.____
B (no3)
G#m7
B (no3) / F#
E 2(no3)
1
CHOIR unis.
SOLO
____ yeah,____________ I'm gon - na be al - right.____ Yeah.____
1
G#m7
E

17
CD: 10
B (no3)
E 2 (no3)
B (no3)/F#
G#m7
B
E 2 (no3)
B (no3)/F#
20
(to pg. 14, meas. 9)
2, 3
We're gon - na
B (no3)/F#
(to pg. 14, meas. 9)
2, 3
G#m7
22
f
SOLO (melody) with CHOIR
be al - right.___ 'Cause I
mel.
know
my___
God___
f
mel.
E
B
f

24
saved the day, and I know His Word
B/E
B(no3)/F#
26
nev-er fails. And I know my God
G#m
B
2nd time to Coda
(to pg. 18, meas. 35)
28
made a way for me.
E
2nd time to Coda
(to pg. 18, meas. 35)
C#m

30
Sal - va - tion___ is___ here.___
E 2
B (no 3)
32
D.S. al Coda
(to pg. 14, meas. 9)
B (no 3)
D.S. al Coda
(to pg. 14, meas. 9)
CODA
CD: 12
35
SOLO cont. with CHOIR
'Cause I know my___ God___
mel.
CODA
C#m
E 2
B

38
saved the day, and I know His Word
B/E
B (no3)/F#
40
nev - er fails. And I know my God
G#m
B
42
made a way for me.
E
C#m

44
Sal - va - tion is here.
E²
G♯m7
46
N.C.
mf
El. Bass cues: bass plays
16th pattern throughout
CD: 13
49
SOLO
mf
52
Sal - va - tion is here.
Sal - va - tion is
G♯m
B
remaining rhythm
gradually enters

55
here and He lives in me. Sal - va - tion is here.
E
C#m
G#m
CD: 14
58
Sal - va - tion that died just to set me free. Sal - va - tion is
CHOIR unis.
mf
Sal - va - tion is
mf
B
E
C#m
grad. building
SOLO with CHOIR
61
here. Sal - va - tion is here and He lives in me.
G#m
B
E

22
64
Sal - va - tion is here. 'Cause You are a - live
C#m
G#m
B
67
and You live in me! Sal - va - tion is here.
mel.
f
mel. f
E
C#m
B
f
70
Sal - va - tion is here and He lives in me. Sal - va - tion is
E
F#
G#m

73
here. 'Cause You are a-live and You live in me!
B
E
F#
76
'Cause I know my God saved the day, and I know
G#m
B
79
His Word nev-er fails. And I know my God
B

82
made a way for me. We're gon - na
B
C#m
84
be al - right. 'Cause I know my God
E
B
86
SOLO may ad lib
saved the day, and I know His Word
B/E
B(no3)/F#

88
nev - er fails. And I know my God
G#m
B
90
made a way for me. Sal - va - tion is
E
C#m
E 2
93
here. Sal - va - tion is here and He lives in me.
B (no 3)
E 2 (no 3)
F#(add4)

26
96
Sal - va - tion is here. 'Cause You are a - live
G#m
B (no3)
E 2(no3)
99
SOLO
and You live in me! Sal - va - tion is here.
F#(add4)
G#m
B (no3)
102
B (no3)

Holy

Words and Music by
ANDREA JONES, RAY JONES
BENJAMIN JONES and CHRISTOPHER JONES
Arr. by Kristen Silvia

CD: 15

Acoustic pop ♩ = ca. 73

SOLO
mp

CD: 16

28
SOLO with CHOIR unis.
mp
Ho - ly___ Ho - ly___ Ho - ly___ God___
mp
E2 B C#m7
Ho - ly___ Ho - ly___
A2 E2 B
CD: 17
Ho - ly___ God___
C#m7 A2

18
SOLO
O my God, how great You are,
E2
B
20
clothed in maj - es - ty.
C#m7
A2
22
Righ - teous One, the Great I AM,
E2
B
24
just and mer - ci - ful.
C#m7
A2

26
You are the One,____ the Ho - ly____ One.____
F#m7
E/G#
A2
B

CD: 18
28
You are the One,____ the Ho - ly____ One._______
C#m7
B/D#

SOLO joins CHOIR
30
mf
Ho - ly____ Ho - ly____
mf
E2
B
mf

32
Ho - ly___ God___ Ho - ly___
C#m7
A2
E2
35
Ho - ly___ Ho - ly___ God___
B
C#m7
A2
38
Je - sus__ Christ,__ the sav - ing__ One,__
E2
B

Li - on and the Lamb.
God and Man, the Ris - en King,
Match - less is Your name.

46
You are the One,___ the Ho - ly___ One.___
F#m7
E/G#
A2
B
CD: 19
48
You are the One,___ the Ho - ly___ One.___
C#m7
B/D#
50
Ho - ly___ Ho - ly___ Ho - ly___ God___
E2
B
C#m7

53
Ho - ly___
Ho - ly___
A2
E2
B
56
Ho - ly___
God___
C#m7
A2
58
SOLO
mp
You are the One,___ the Ho - ly___ One.___
F#m7
E/G#
A2
B
mp

60
You are the One,___ the Ho - ly___ One.___
C#m7
B/D#

SOLO joins CHOIR
62
mf
You are the One,___ the Ho - ly___ One.___
mf
F#m7
E/G#
A2
B
mf

64
You are the One,___ the Ho - ly___ One.___
C#m7
B/D#

66
You are the One,___ the Ho - ly___ One.___
F#m7
E/G#
A2
B
68
CD: 20
You are the One,___ the Ho - ly___ One.___
C#m7
B/D#
1st time: SOLO sings melody with CHOIR
2nd time: SOLO sings part as written
70
You are the One, the ho - ly Lord, You are the
Ho - ly___ Ho - ly___ Ho - ly___ God___
E2
B
C#m7

73
One who saves us. You are the One, the ho - ly
Ho - ly Ho - ly
A2 E2 B
76
(to pg. 36, meas. 70)
God, You are the God who saves.
(to pg. 36, meas. 70)
Ho - ly God
C#m7 A2 (to pg. 36, meas. 70)

78
SOLO ad lib with CHOIR
You are the One,___ the Ho - ly___ One.___ You are the One,___ the
F#m7   E/G#   A2   B   C#m7
81
Ho - ly___ One.______ You are the One,___ the Ho - ly___ One.___
B/D#   F#m7   E/G#   A2   B
84
You are the One,___ the Ho - ly___ One.___
C#m7   B

Glorified

Words and Music by
JARED ANDERSON
Arr. by Kristen Silvia

Solid, driving ♩ = ca. 85

CD: 22
CHOIR unis. with SOLO
Praise be-longs to You.
What can I do but sing?
The great-est joy I've found
is to lay a crown be-fore my King,
be-fore my King.

CD: 23
CHOIR with SOLO on melody
I've come to wor - ship;
I've come to lift up Your name, for You de - serve ___ this
life laid down like the one that You gave. I have but one voice,
D² A F♯m⁷ E D A
F♯m⁷ E D A
F♯m⁷ E D A

42
26
one heart and one sac-ri-fice. So would You take___ this
F#m7   E   D   A
28
life laid down and be glo-ri-fied?___ Be glo-ri-fied._
F#m7   E   D2   A   E   F#m7
2nd time to Coda
(to pg. 45, meas. 49)
CD: 24 1st time
31
mf
Praise be-longs to You;
mf
2nd time to Coda
(to pg. 45, meas. 49)
D   A   E   D2   A
mf

34
let songs from chil - dren rise.
You si - lence all Your foes;
F#m7
E
D2
A
36
You set Your glo - ry in the skies.
F#m7
E
D2
A
F#m7
E
SOLO
mp
39
Praise be - longs to You;
D2
A
F#m7
E
D
A
mp

42
cre - a - tion's call - ing now   for the King to be re - vealed;
F♯m7   E   D   A
44
mf
O, King of heav-en come down,___   King of heav-en___ come___
mf
King of heav-en___ come___
mf
F♯m7   E   D   A   F♯m7   E
mf

47
D.S. al Coda
(to pg. 41, meas. 21)
down.
D.S. al Coda
(to pg. 41, meas. 21)
down.
D   A   F♯m7   E
D.S. al Coda
(to pg. 41, meas. 21)
CODA
49
Be glo-ri-fied,   be glo-ri-fied.
CODA
F♯m7   E   D2   A   E   F♯m7

52
SOLO ad lib
D
A
E
D
CD: 25
55
E/D
D
E/D
SOLO and CHOIR unis.
(Hand claps on beats 2 & 4)
58
I've come to wor - ship; I've come to lift up Your name,
Drums only

CD: 26
60
for You de - serve — this life laid down like the one that You gave.
62
I have but one voice, one heart and one sac - ri - fice. So would You take — this
65
SOLO
life laid down and be glo - ri - fied? Would You be glo - ri - fied? —
life laid down and be glo - ri - fied. —
D   A   E   F#m7
f

68
Be glo-ri-fied.
Be glo-ri-fied,
D   A   E   F#m7   D   A
71
Would You be glo-ri-fied?
be glo-ri-fied.   Be glo-ri-fied.
E   F#m7   D   A   E   F#m7

74
I've come to wor - ship; I've come to lift up Your name,
be glo - ri - fied.
D   A   E   F#m7
76
for You de - serve this life laid down like the one that You gave.
be glo - ri - fied.
D   A   E   F#m7

78
I have but one voice, one heart and one sac - ri - fice.
be glo - ri - fied.
D
A
E
F♯m7
80
So would You take___ this life laid down and be glo - ri - fied?_____
D
A
E

Worthy Are You Lord

Words and Music by
BRYAN SILVIA
and KRISTEN SILVIA
Arr. by Kristen Silvia

7
An - cient of Days. Great is the Lord;
An - cient of Days. Great is the Lord;
C#m7 B sus A sus C#m7 B sus
10
CD: 28 1st time
1st time: DUET
mf
our hands we raise. You are high
our hands we raise. You are high
A2 C#m7 B sus A2

53
13
and ex-al - ted. You are ev - 'ry-thing_ I need._
and ex-al - ted._ You are ev - 'ry-thing_ I need._
E
B/D#
A
2nd time, more driving
CD: 29 1st time
16
You are high____ and ex-al - ted, so I lift_
You are high____ and ex-al - ted,_ so I lift_
A
F#m7(4)
E
B/D#

19
my voice and sing. Wor - thy are You, Lord.
Both times: CHOIR
my voice and sing. Wor - thy are You, Lord.
A 2
A
21
SOLOS and DUET join CHOIR
You gave Your life for me. So I will give my ev -
E
B

23
-'ry-thing to You. Wor-thy are You, Lord.
C#m7   B sus   A2
25
You came to set me free. So I will live my life
E
B/D#
27
to speak Your truth. Wor-thy are You, Lord.
C#m7   B sus   A2

29
1
CD: 30
(to pg. 51, meas. 5)
2
C#m7   B(add4)   A2   E
32
CD: 31
SOLO
Wor-thy are You, Lord.
B/D#
C#m7   B(add4)   A2

One day ev - 'ry knee will bow
One day ev - 'ry knee will bow
and the heav - ens will pro - claim
and the heav - ens will pro - claim
F#m7
A2
F#m7
B sus
35
37

39
that You a - lone_ are God.______
that You a - lone_ are God._
F#m7
A2
CD: 32
41
And for - e - ver You_ will reign!______
You____ will____ reign!
F#m7
B sus

43
mp
Wor - thy are You, Lord. You gave Your life for me.
B
E
mp
45
So I will give my ev - 'ry - thing to You.
B
C#m7
B(add4)
47
DUET
Wor - thy are You, Lord. You came to set me free.
A2
E

49
So I will live__ my life______ to speak__ Your truth.__
B
C#m7
B(add4)

51
BOTH continue unis.
You are high______ and ex - al -
Wor - thy are__ You, Lord.______ You gave Your life__ for me.__
A2
E

53
ted. You are e - 'ry-thing_ I need._
So I will give_ my ev - 'ry-thing_ to_ You._
B
C#m7
B sus
55
You are high_ and ex - al -
Wor - thy are_ You, Lord._ You came to set_ me free.
A 2
E

57
- ted, so I lift my voice and sing.
So I will live my life to speak Your truth.
B/D#
C#m7
B sus
59
Wor - thy are You, Lord.
Wor - thy are You, Lord.
A 2
E 2

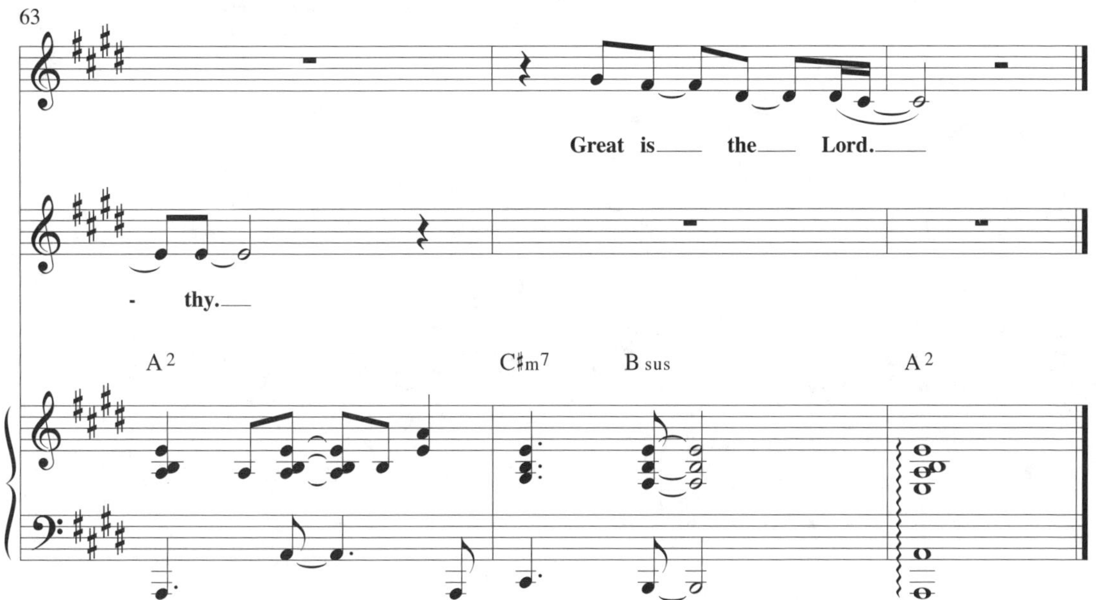

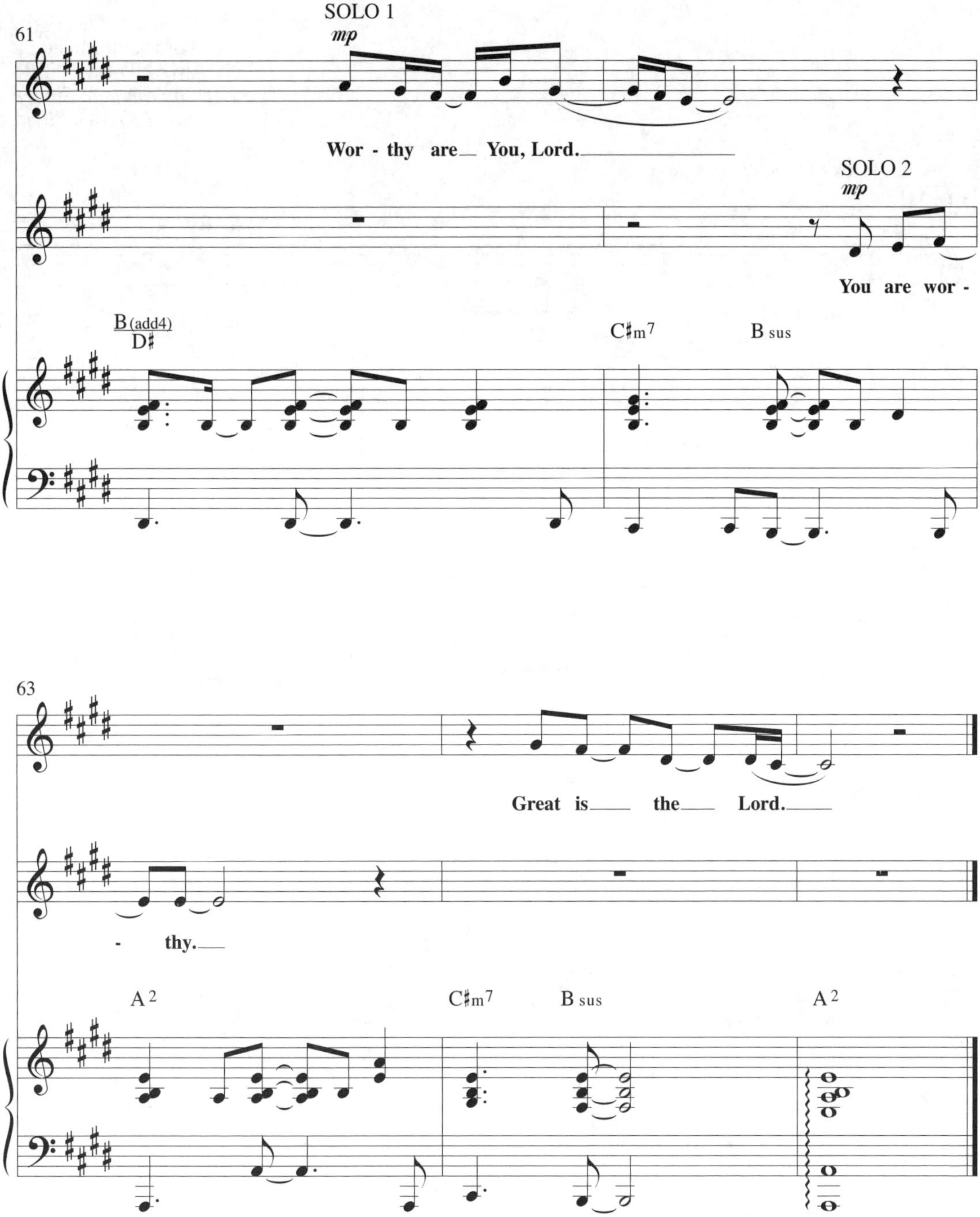
61
SOLO 1
mp
Wor - thy are You, Lord.
SOLO 2
mp
You are wor -
B(add4)/D♯
C♯m7
B sus
63
Great is the Lord.
- thy.
A2
C♯m7
B sus
A2

Knocking at the Door

Words and Music by
AMANDA SINGER
*Arr. by Amanda Singer
and Kristen Silvia*

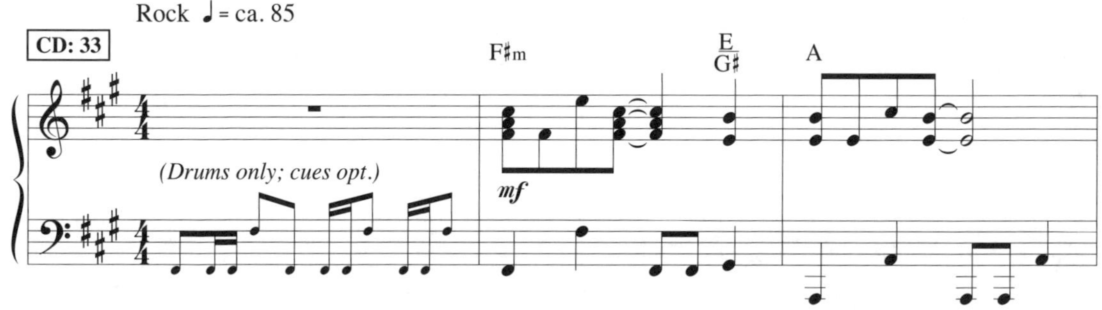

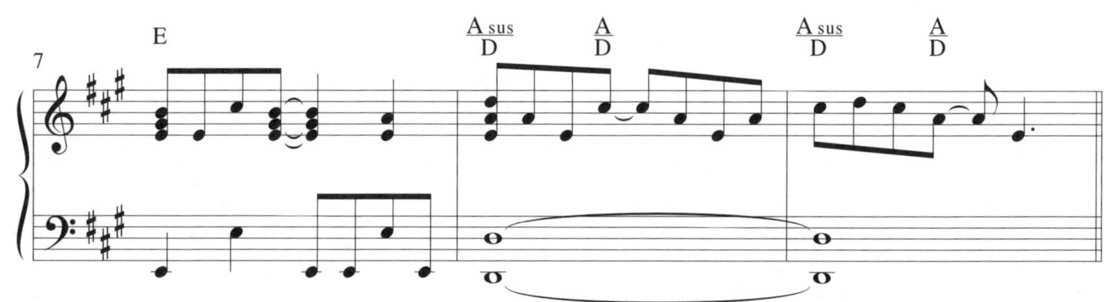

© 2011 Pilot Point Music/ASCAP (admin. by Music Services).
All rights reserved.

1st time: SOLO
mf 2nd time: CHOIR unis. (Solo ad lib freely)
10
1. Knock - in' at the door of the Ho - ly of ho - lies;
2. Knock - in' at the door of the Ho - ly of ho - lies;
mf
F#m7
A
12
Je - sus it's Your blood that lets me in.
I sur - ren - der, Lord; I've had e - nough.
B m7
D M9
14
Though I don't de - serve to be in Your pre - sence,
Ev - en though I come wound - ed and wea - ry;
F#m7
A

16
You will meet_ me there_ and take_ my sin._
Be - ing here_ with You_ will lift_ me up._
D M7
CD: 34 1st time
18
1st time: SOLO (Top notes)
Make me ho - ly as You're ho - ly.
D
E/D
D
E/D
1st time: DUET
2nd time: CHOIR
20
O God,_ I want_ to be_ with You._
A
E
D
E

22
This world_ has noth-ing for_____ me.____
F#m7   C#m   Bm7
24
O God,_ I long_ to lose_____ my-self_ in You.____
A   E   D   E
26
This world_ has noth-ing for_____ me.____
F#m7   C#m   G2

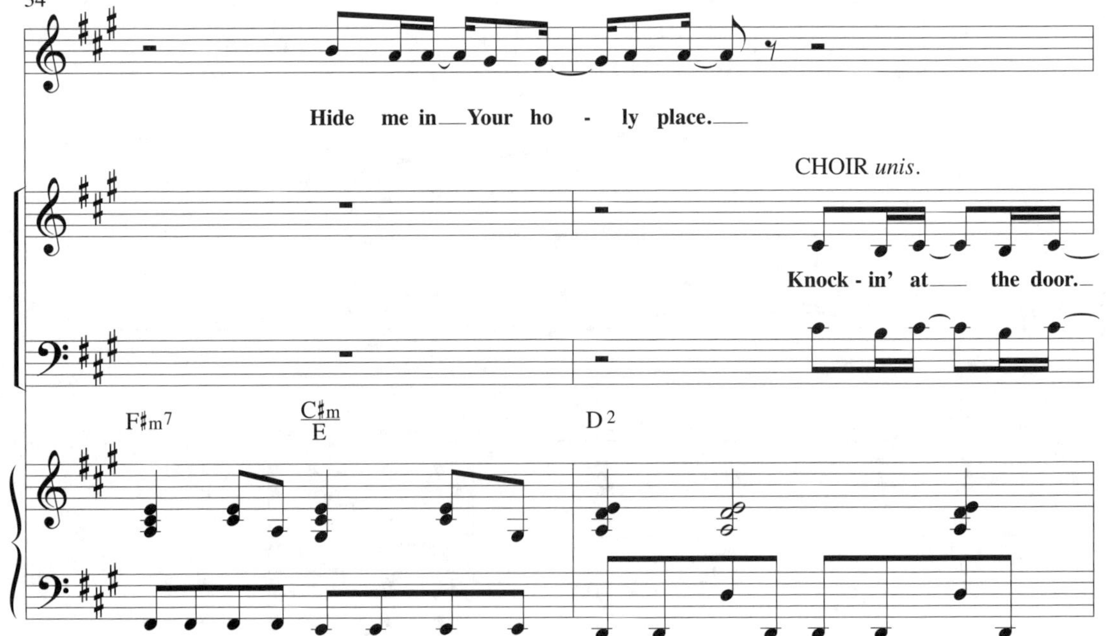

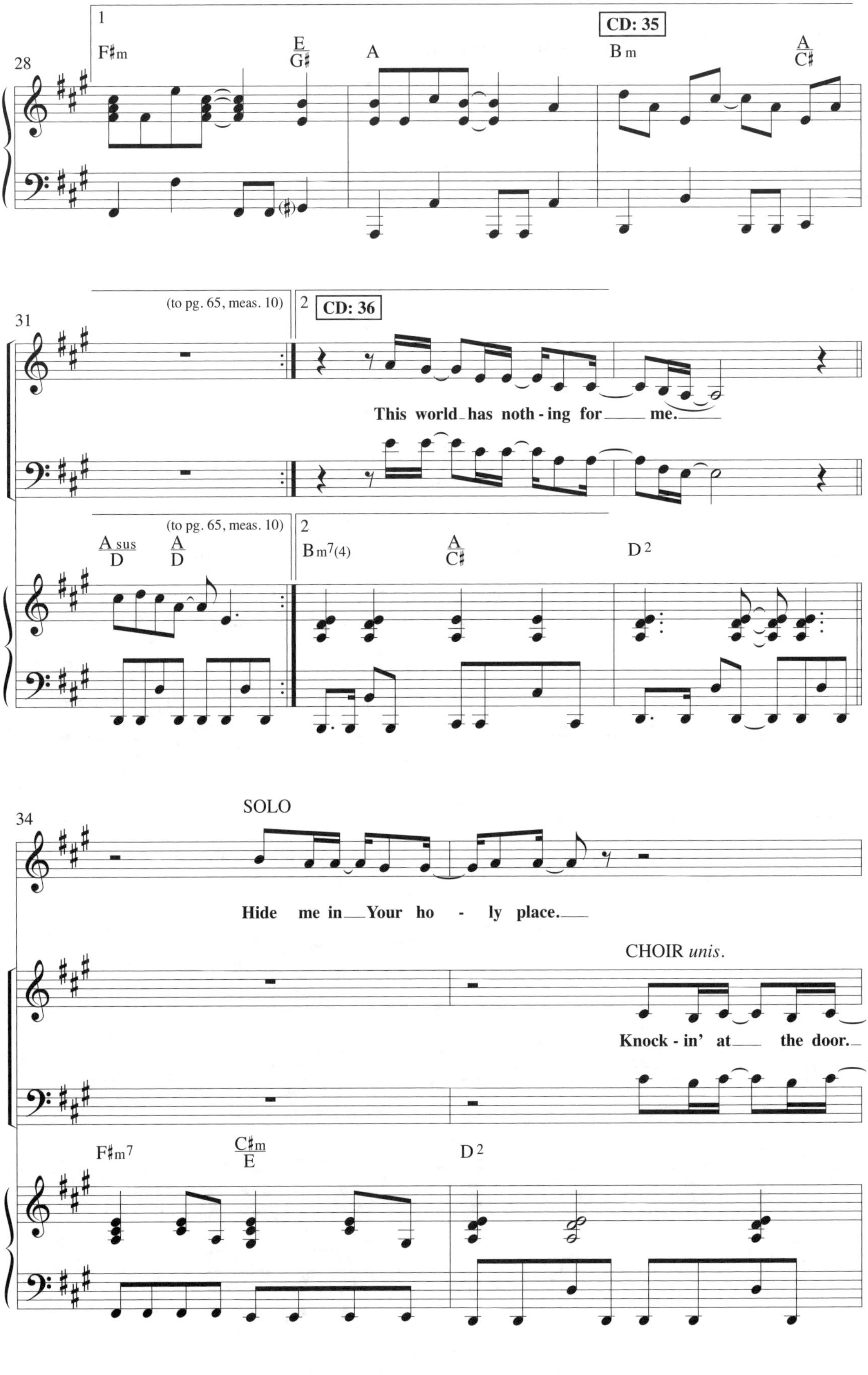
CD: 35
F♯m
E/G♯
A
Bm
A/C♯
(to pg. 65, meas. 10)
CD: 36
This world has noth - ing for me.
Asus/D
A/D
Bm7(4)
A/C♯
D2
SOLO
Hide me in Your ho - ly place.
CHOIR unis.
Knock - in' at the door.
F♯m7
C♯m/E
D2

36
Hide me in Your love.
Bm7
A2/E
D2
38
Hide me in Your ho - ly place.
Knock - in' at the door;
F#m7
C#m/E
D2

40
Hide me in Your love.
love!
B m7
A2/E
G2(6)
42
SOLO
O God, I want to be with You.
N.C.
44
This world has noth-in' for me.

46
CHOIR parts
O God,__ I long__ to lose__ my-self__ in You.__
A
E
D
E
48
This world__ has noth - ing for__ me.__
F#m7
C#m
G2
SOLO may ad lib to end
50
This world__ has noth - in' for__ me.__
Bm7
A/C#
DM9

52
F#m7
C#m7
A/D
This world__ has noth - in' for ____ me. __

54
B m7
C#m7
D M9
This world__ has noth - in' for ____ me. __

56
F#m7
C#m
D M9
This world__ has noth - in' for____ me.____

58
SOLO only
This world_ has noth - in' for_______ me._______
G 2

Top of Our Lungs

Words and Music by
**ADRIAN BRADFORD,
JON NEUFELD and TIM NEUFELD**
Arr. by Kristen Silvia

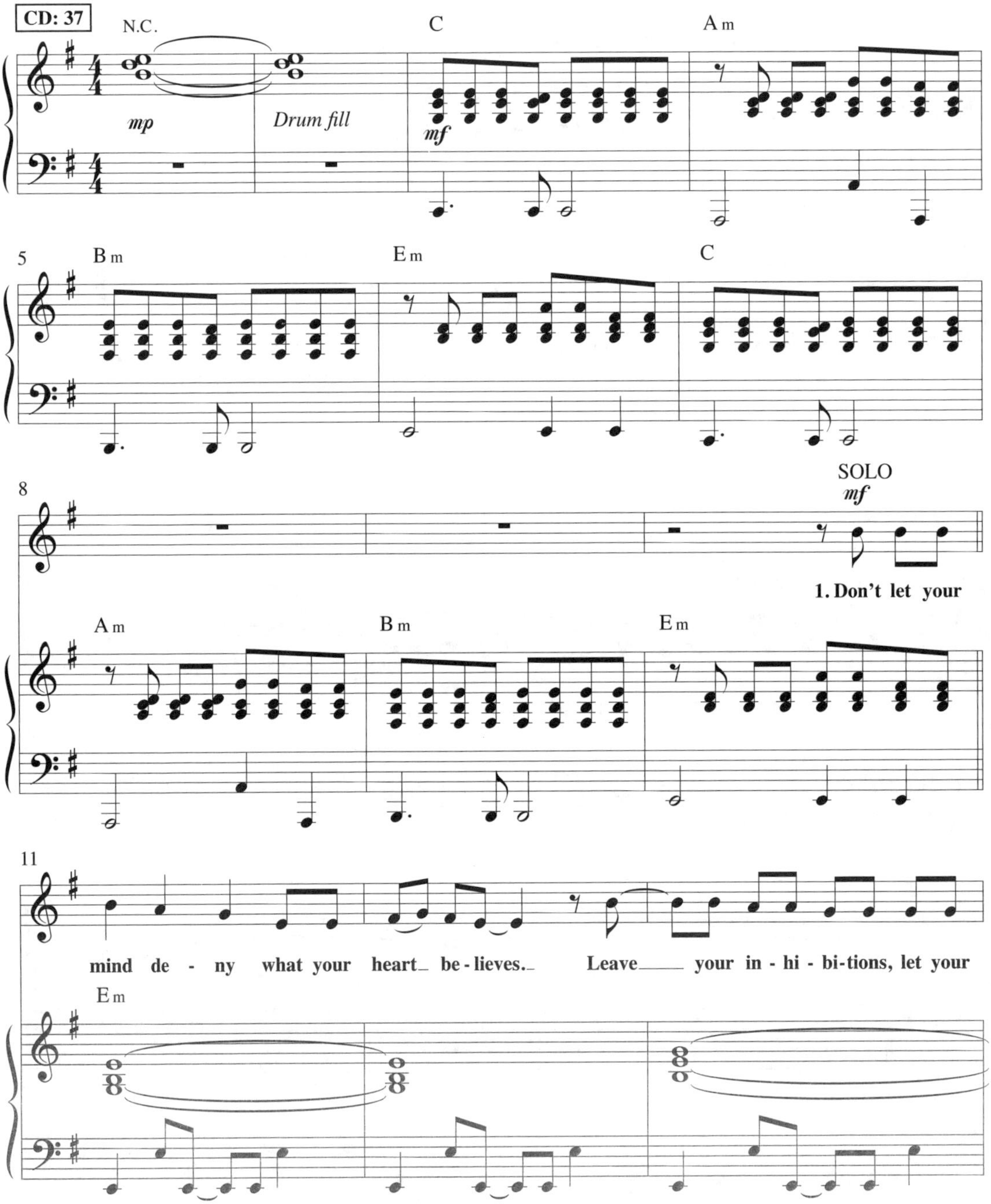

14
soul be free. This is why you were cre - a - ted; it's your des - ti - ny. It's al - right,
CHOIR unis.
mf
It's al - right,
mf
Em
17
it's al - right, it's al - right. Who the Son sets free,
it's al - right, it's al - right.
Em
CM7

20
DUET
(Male)
mf
(Female)
yeah, they are free___ in - deed;___ So___ let go___
D
A sus
E
23
CD: 38
___ with me,___ come on and sing what you___ be - lieve.___
C M7
D
A m
26
___ We're gon - na shout His praise at the top of our lungs. We're gon - na
CHOIR parts
We're gon - na shout His praise at the top of our lungs. We're gon - na
A m
A m
C
A m
B sus
E m

29
dance for the glo - ry of the ris - en Son. We're not a -
dance for the glo - ry of the ris - en Son. We're not a -
C   Am   Bsus   Em
31
shamed, not a-shamed of the One we love. We're gon - na shout His praise at the
shamed, not a-shamed of the One we love. We're gon - na shout His praise at the
C   Am   Bsus   Em   C   Am

CD: 39
top of our lungs.
2. This is the
top of our lungs.
2. This is the
B sus
E m
SOLO with CHOIR
praise of a peo-ple that have been re-deemed. This is the joy of the Lord and the
E m
sound of the free. This is why we were cre-a-ted, it's our
E m

42
(Solo only)
des - ti - ny. It's al-right, it's al-right, it's al-right._____ Who the
Em

45
Son_____ sets free,_____ yeah they are free_ in - deed;_
Son_____ sets free,_____ yeah they are free_ in - deed;_
C M7
D
A sus

48
So let go with me, come on and
So let go with me, come on and
E
CM7
D
CD: 40
51
sing what you be - lieve. We're gon - na shout His praise at the
sing what you be - lieve. We're gon - na shout His praise at the
Am
C
Am

54
top of our lungs. We're gon - na dance for the glo - ry of the
top of our lungs. We're gon - na dance for the glo - ry of the
B sus   Em   C   Am
56
ris - en Son. We're not a - shamed, not a-shamed of the One we love. We're gon - na
ris - en Son. We're not a - shamed, not a-shamed of the One we love. We're gon - na
B sus   Em   C   Am   B sus   Em

59
shout His praise at the top of our lungs.
shout His praise at the top of our lungs.
C   Am   Bsus   Em   C
62   D   Bm   Em
CD: 41
65   C   D   Bm

Male SOLO
We're gon - na shout His praise at the
top of our lungs. We're gon - na dance for the glo - ry of the
Female SOLO
Top of our lungs,
ris - en Son. We're not a - shamed, not a - shamed of the
ris - en Son.

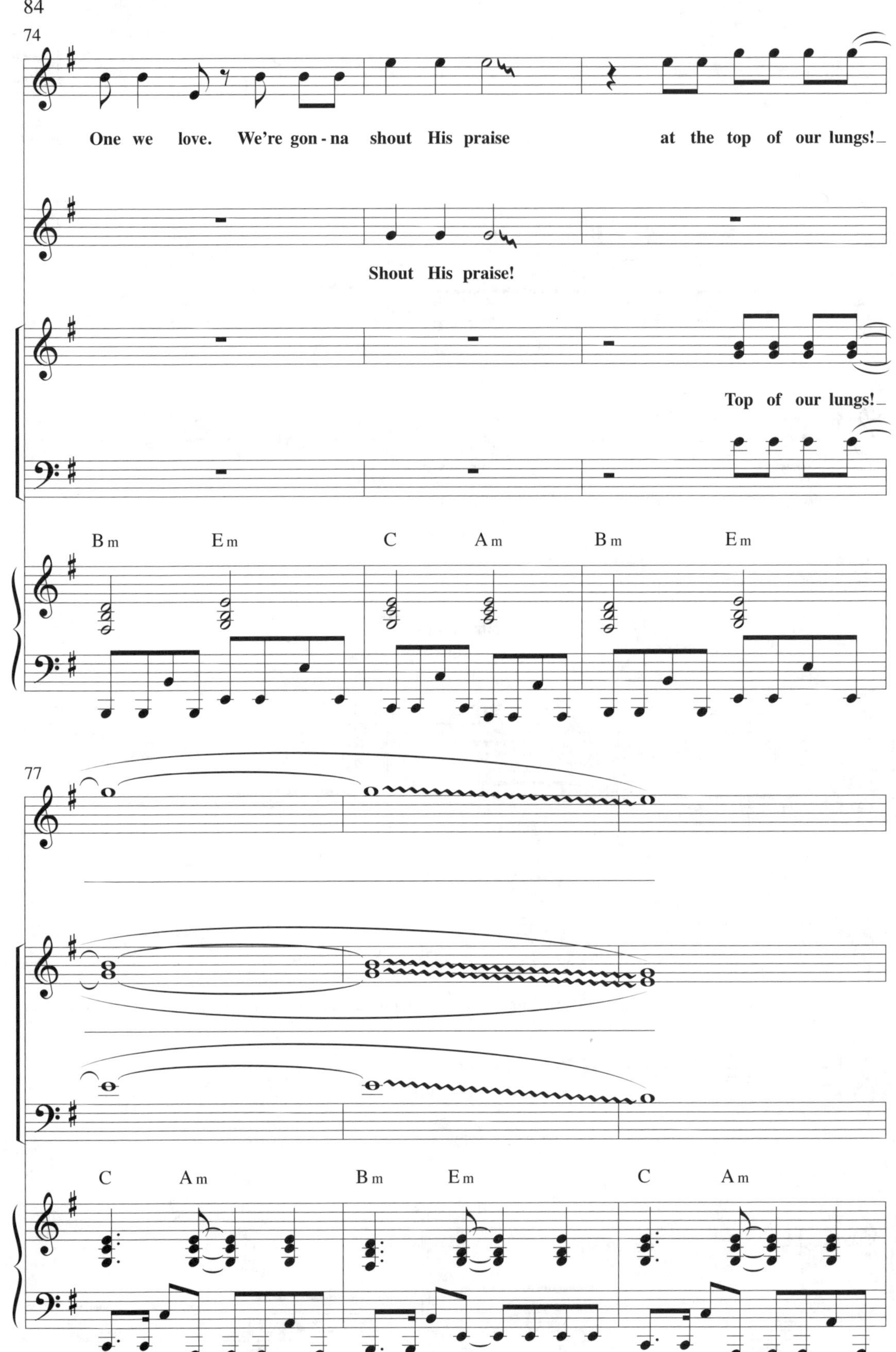
One we love. We're gon-na shout His praise at the top of our lungs!
Shout His praise!
Top of our lungs!
B m   E m   C   A m   B m   E m
C   A m   B m   E m   C   A m

80
SOLOS join CHOIR
We're gon - na shout His praise at the
B m   E m   C   A m
82
top of our lungs. We're gon - na dance for the glo - ry of the
B m   E m   C   A m
84
ris - en Son. We're not a - shamed, not a - shamed of the
B m   E m   C   A m

One we love. We're gon-na shout His praise at the
top of our lungs.

Oh the Blood

Words and Music by
JOSH LOPEZ
Arr. by Kristen Silvia

10
You took from me,— deep-er is Your love still.
F#m7
C#m
A
13
Strong-er than an-y sin, grace nev-er end-ing. Your love is
E2
F#m7
C#m
16
CD: 44 2nd time
o - ver-tak - ing me. You took my
CHOIR unis. (2nd time only)
You took my
A
C#m
B

CD: 43 1st time
19
sin and gave me life.
sin and gave me life.
E   C#m   B   A
22
Oh, the blood You shed for me, washed
CHOIR unis.
mf
Oh, the blood You shed for me, washed
mf
E   B   C#m

25
all my sin. Oh, the cross You
all my sin. Oh, the cross You
A E B
28
car - ried for me and died my death. Oh, the
car - ried for me and died my death. Oh, the
(to pg. 87, meas. 5)
2
C#m A E

31
blood You shed for me, washed all my sin.
blood You shed for me, washed all my sin.
B
C#m
A
34
Oh, the cross You car - ried for me and
Oh, the cross You car - ried for me and
E
B
C#m

died my death. Oh, the nails
died my death. Oh, the nails
A   E   B
driv-en to take all my shame. Oh, the
driv-en to take all my shame. Oh, the
C#m   A   E

43
grave___ is emp-ty be-cause___ You are a-live,___ Je -
grave___ is emp-ty be-cause___ You are a-live,___ Je -
B   C#m   A
46
sus.___
sus.___
C#m   B   E

49
A 2
C#m
B
CD: 45
52
SOLO
mp
Sin has no more pow'r;   You broke ev-'ry chain.
E
A 2
C#m
B
mp
56
I'm a-live_ be-cause You_ con-quered the grave._   Sin has no more pow'r;
CHOIR unis.
Sin has no more pow'r;
Sin has no more pow'r;
E
A
C#m

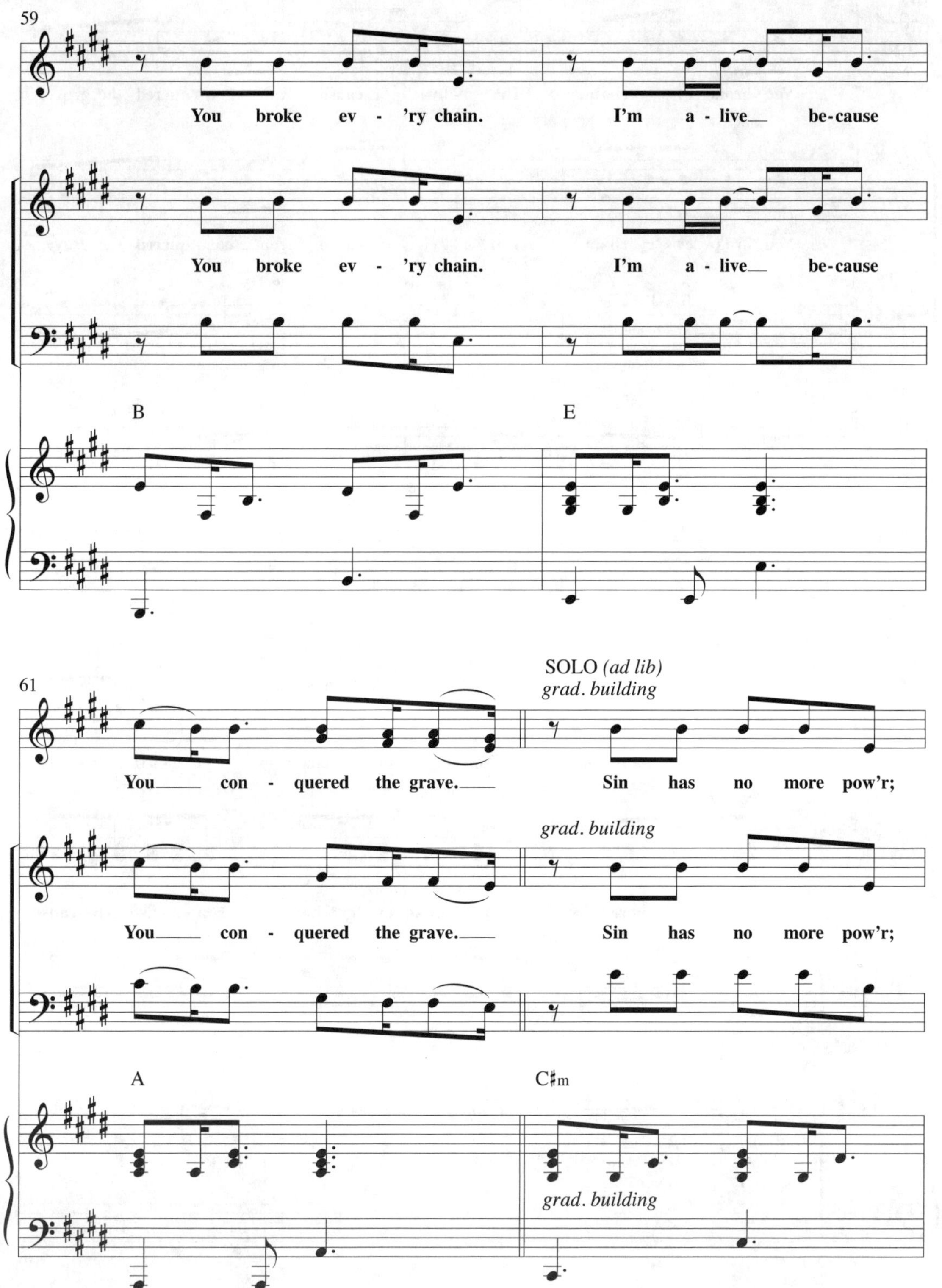
59
You broke ev - 'ry chain.
I'm a - live___ be-cause
You broke ev - 'ry chain.
I'm a - live___ be-cause
B
E
61
SOLO (ad lib)
grad. building
You___ con - quered the grave.___
Sin has no more pow'r;
grad. building
You___ con - quered the grave.___
Sin has no more pow'r;
A
C#m
grad. building

63
CD: 46
You broke ev - 'ry chain.
I'm a - live__ be-cause
You__ con - quered the grave.__
You broke ev - 'ry chain.
I'm a - live__ be-cause
You__ con - quered the grave.__
B
E
A
(Solo may ad lib)
66
mf - f
Sin has no more pow'r;
You broke ev - 'ry chain.
I'm a - live__ be-cause
mf - f
Sin has no more pow'r;
You broke ev - 'ry chain.
I'm a - live__ be-cause
mf - f
C#m
B
E
mf - f

69
1
(to pg. 96, meas. 66)
2
You con - quered the grave. You con - quered the grave.
1
(to pg. 96, meas. 66)
2
You con - quered the grave. You con - quered the grave.
1
(to pg. 96, meas. 66)
2
A2
A2
71
Oh, the blood You
Oh, the blood You
A2
E
B

74
shed for me, washed all my sin. Oh,_______ the
shed for me, washed all my sin. Oh,_______ the
C#m
A
E
77
cross________ You car-ried for me__ and died my death.
cross________ You car-ried for me__ and died my death.
B
C#m
A

80
Oh, the nails driv-en to take
Oh, the nails driv-en to take
E
B
C#m
83
all my shame. Oh, the grave is emp-ty be-cause
all my shame. Oh, the grave is emp-ty be-cause
A
E
B
C#m

87
CD: 47
You are a - live__ Je - sus.
You are a - live__ Je - sus.
A
C#m
B
90
DUET
Je - sus!
E
A2
C#m
93
B
E
A2

96
SOLOS may ad lib
Sin has no more pow'r; You broke ev - 'ry chain.
Sin has no more pow'r; You broke ev - 'ry chain.
C#m
B
98
I'm a - live__ be-cause You__ con - quered the grave.__
I'm a - live__ be-cause You__ con - quered the grave.__
E
A 2

100
Sin has no more pow'r; You broke ev - 'ry chain. I'm a - live_ be - cause
Sin has no more pow'r; You broke ev - 'ry chain. I'm a - live_ be - cause
C#m
B
E
103
DUET
mf
You____ con - quered the grave.____ Sin has no more pow'r;
You____ con - quered the grave.____
A 2
C#m
mf

105
B
You broke ev - 'ry chain.
E
I'm a - live__ be-cause

SOLO
mp
107
You__ con - quered the grave.__
A2
Sin has no more pow'r;
C#m
mp
You broke ev - 'ry chain.
B

110
rit.
I'm a - live__ be-cause
E
You__ con - quered the grave.__
A2
rit.

My Jesus, I Love Thee

WILLIAM R. FEATHERSTONE,
BRYAN SILVIA and KRISTEN SILVIA

ADONIRAM J. GORDAN,
BRYAN SILVIA and KRISTEN SILVIA
*Arr. by Kristen Silvia
and Mark Martin*

1st time: CHOIR (unis.)
2nd time: SOLO
mf
(1.) Je - sus, I love Thee; I know Thou art
2. love Thee be - cause Thou has first lov - ed
D   D sus   B m   A sus   A
mf
mine. For Thee all the fol - lies of
me, And pur - chased my par - don on
G   D   D sus   B m
sin I re - sign. My gra - cious Re -
Cal - va - ry's tree. I love Thee for
A sus   A   G   D

19
deem - er, my Sav - ior art Thou: If
wear - ing the thorns on Thy brow: If
Em
G
A sus
CD: 50 2nd time
22
ev - er I loved Thee, my Je - sus, 'tis
ev - er I loved Thee, my Je - sus, 'tis
D 2
B m
A sus
25
1
now.
1 G
D
B m
(Piano cues)

28
CD: 49
(to pg. 105, meas. 10)
SOLO mf
2
2. I   now.
A sus
G 2
G 2
31
CHOIR parts
I   love   ev - er - y - thing_ that You are.___   Lord,
mel.
A
D
A
34
CD: 52 2nd time
You are my King._ Je - sus, You___   are   all that I need_ and I love_
D
A
B m

37
CD: 51 1st time
1st time: SOLO freely
2nd time: CHOIR unis.
___ You.   Lord, I love___You.___   3. I'll love   Thee in
4. In   man - sions of
A   G   D   D sus
40
life,___   I will   love   Thee   in   death.   And
glo - ry and   end - less   de - light,   I'll
B m   A sus   A   G
43
praise   Thee   as   long___   as   Thou   lend - est   me
ev - er   a - dore___   Thee   in   heav - en   so
D   D sus   B m   A sus   A

46
breath. And say when the death dew lies
bright. I'll say sing with the glit - ter - ing
G
D/F#
Em
49
cold on my brow, "If ev - er I
crown on my brow, "If ev - er I
G
A sus
D 2
52
1 (to pg. 107, meas. 31)
loved Thee, my Je - sus, 'tis now."
loved Thee, my
Bm
1 (to pg. 107, meas. 31)
A sus
G 2

55
2
Je - sus, 'tis now. If ev - er I
2
A sus
G 2
D 2
58
loved_____ Thee, my Je - sus, 'tis now, my
B m
A sus
G 2
61
Je - sus, 'tis now."
G 2
D 2

Song of Hope

Words and Music by
ANDREA JONES, RAY JONES,
BENJAMIN JONES and CHRISTOPHER JONES
Arr. by Kristen Silvia

10
emp - ty,___ I cry out___ in prayer.___
Sav - ior,___ for lov - ing me.___
Em
D
C2
13
Out of___ the dark - ness,___ in - to___ the light,___
Out of___ the dark - ness,___ in - to___ the light,___
G
Em
D
CD: 54 1st time
CD: 56 2nd time
16
___ I called and___ You___ an - swered,___
___ I called and___ You___ an - swered,___
C2
G
Em

19
gave me___ new life.___
gave me___ new life.___
God is my rock,___ my for-tress, my ref-
D
C²
22
-uge; reached down from on high___ and res-cued me.___
G
C²
24
He is my shield___ in times of trou-
E m²
C²

26
1st time: GIRLS unis.
2nd time: CHOIR unis.
1
- ble.
My God____ de - liv - ers me.____
G/B
1
C2
D
G
29
CD: 55
(to pg. 111, meas. 5)
CHOIR unis. mf
2. You
C2
G
C2
(to pg. 111, meas. 5)
32
2
CD: 57
____ de - liv - ers me.____
My God____ de - liv - ers me!____
2 C
D
Em2
C2
D

35
3rd time: SOLO may ad lib
f
I will call upon the Lord, who is wor-
G
C²
G/B
38
-thy to be praised. I am saved from all my en-
C²
G/B
C²
D
41
4th time to Coda
(to pg. 118, meas. 61)
1, 3
(to meas. 36)
-e-mies, my ref-uge and my song. I will call
4th time to Coda
(to pg. 118, meas. 61)
1, 3
(to meas. 36)
Em
C²
D
G

44
CD: 58
-fuge and my song, my ref - uge and my song!
C2   D   Em   C2   D
1st time: SOLO
2nd time: GIRLS unis.
mp
47
God is my rock, my for-tress, my ref-
G   C2
2nd time: more motion
50
-uge; reached down from on high and res - cued me.
G   C2   D

52
GIRLS unis. both times
Em
C2
G/B
He is my shield___ in times of trou - ble. My God___
55
1
(to pg. 116, meas. 49)
2
de - liv - ers me.___ God is my rock,___ ___ de - liv - ers me.___
1
C2
D
G
(to pg. 116, meas. 49)
2
C2
D
D.S. al Coda
(to pg. 115, meas. 36)
CHOIR parts
cresc.
f
58
My God___ de - liv - ers me!___ I will call___
f
D.S. al Coda
(to pg. 115, meas. 36)
Em
C2
D
G

CODA
61
- fuge____ and____ my   song,____   my ref -
CODA
C2   D   Em

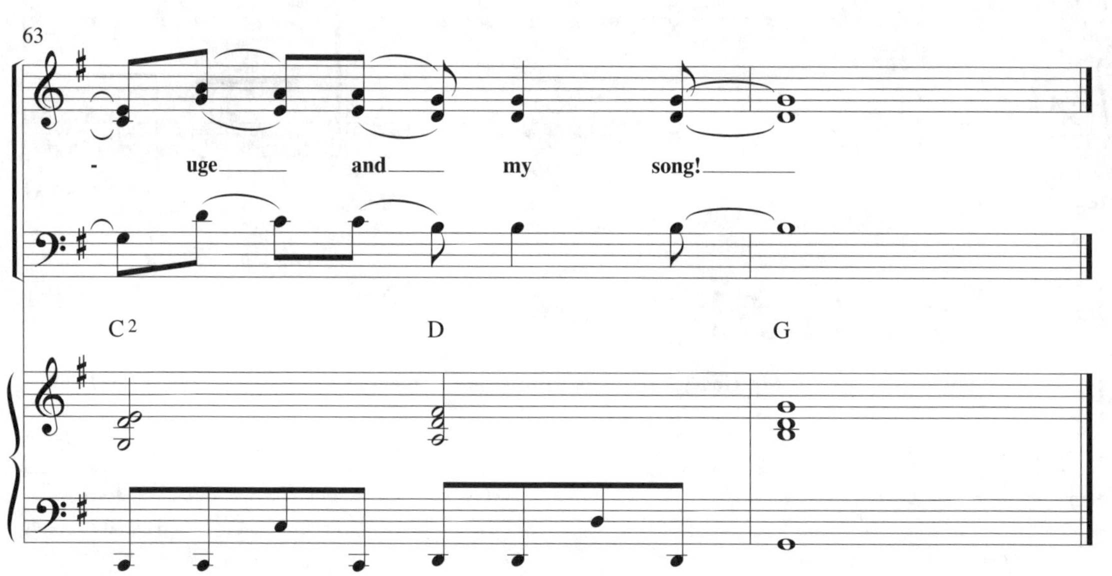

63
- uge____ and____ my   song!____
C2   D   G

How He Loves

Words and Music by
JOHN MARK McMILLIAN
Arr. by Kristen Silvia

Copyright © 2005 Integrity's Hosanna! Music (ASCAP)
(adm. at EMICMGPublishing.com)
All rights reserved. Used by permission.

10
He loves like a hur - ri-cane, I am a tree
B
G#m7
CD: 62 2nd time
13
bend-ing be-neath the weight of His wind and mer - cy.
F#
E2
2nd time: Solo may sing opt. cues
16
All of a sud-den, I am un - a-ware of these af-
E2
B

19
flic - tions e - clipsed by glo - ry. And I re - al - ize just how
G#m7
F#
CD: 60 1st time
2nd time to Coda
(to pg. 123, meas. 41)
22
beau - ti - ful You are and how great Your af - fec - tions are for me.
F#
E2
2nd time to Coda
(to pg. 123, meas. 41)
CHOIR unis. both times (with Solo)
mp
25
Oh, how He loves us so.
mp
B
G#m7

28
Oh, how He loves us. How He loves us
G#m7
F#
31
so.
SOLO may ad lib
E 2
mf
B
34
B
G#m7
F#
CD: 61
38
F#
E
D.S. al Coda
(to pg. 119, meas. 9)

CODA
SOLO cont. singing mel. with CHOIR
for me. Yeah, He loves us. Oh, how He
mel.
CODA
E2
B
loves us. Oh, how He loves us.
G#m7
F#
Oh, how He loves! Yeah, He
F#
E2
1 (to meas. 42)
1 (to meas. 42)

50
SOLO may ad lib during instrumental interlude
2
E2
B
53
G#m7
F#
CD: 63
56
F#
E
59
SOLO
mp
3. We are His por-tion and He is our prize,_ drawn to re-demp-tion by the
B
mp
G#m7

62
grace   in His eyes.   If His grace   is an   o - cean, we're all
G#m7   F#
65
mf
sink - ing.   Heav-en meets earth like an
E2   B
mf
68
sub. f
un-fore-seen kiss. My heart turns vio-lent-ly in - side of my chest.___ I
B   G#m7
sub. f
71
don't have time___ to main - tain these re - grets___when I   think a-bout   the way___
F#   E2
building

74
That He loves us. Oh, how He
f
He loves us. Oh, how He
f
E2
B
f
SOLO with CHOIR
77
loves us. Oh, how He loves us.
G#m7
F#
80
Oh, how He loves! Yeah, He
1 (to meas. 75)
F#
E2
1 (to meas. 75)

1st time: CHOIR and SOLO
2nd time: SOLO ad lib
Oh, how He loves us so.
Oh, how He loves us. How He loves us
so. so.
(to meas. 84)
(to meas. 84)